GYMNASTICS

Gymnastics Training and Fitness

Being Your Best

by Jen Jones

Consultant
Connie Dickson, Minnesota State Chair
USA Gymnastics Women's Program

Capstone press®

Mankato, Minnesota

Snap Books are published by Capstone Press,
151 Good Counsel Drive, P.O. Box 669, Mankato, Minnesota 56002.
www.capstonepress.com

Library of Congress Cataloging-in-Publication Data
Jones, Jen, 1976–
    Gymnastics training and fitness : being your best / by Jen Jones.
    p. cm.—(Snap books. Gymnastics)
    Summary: "A guide for children and pre-teens on ways to train and
keep fit for gymnastics"—Provided by publisher.
    Includes bibliographical references and index.
    ISBN-13: 978-0-7368-6471-8 (hardcover)
    ISBN-10: 0-7368-6471-7 (hardcover)
    1. Gymnastics—Juvenile literature. 2. Physical education and
training—Study and teaching (Elementary) I. Title. II. Series.
GV461.J675 2007
796.44—dc22
                                   2006002802

Editor: Wendy Dieker
Designer: Jennifer Bergstrom
Photo Researcher/Photo Editor: Kelly Garvin

Photo Credits: AP/Wide World Photos/Susan Walsh, 28–29; Capstone Press/Karon Dubke, cover, 3 (all), 4–5, 8–9, 10–11, 12, 13 (both), 14–15 (both), 27; Corbis/Artiga Photo, 16–17 (girl); Corbis/Rick Gomez, 19; Corbis/Tom Stewart, 25; Corbis/zefa/M. Pedone, 20–21; Jennifer Jones, 32; Masterfile/Brian Pieters, 6–7; Shutterstock/bluestocking, 3 (orange), 26 (orange); Shutterstock/Joseph, 23 (banana); Shutterstock/Jostein Hauge, 17 (dumbbells); Shutterstock/Olga Shelego, 24; Shutterstock/Roslen Mack, 3 (grapes), 26 (grapes); Shutterstock/Scott Sanders, 23 (almonds); Shutterstock/Tihis, 23 (strawberries); SuperStock/age fotostock, 22–23 (girl)

Capstone Press thanks the staff and gymnasts at the Mankato Area Gymnastics School, Mankato, Minnesota, for their assistance with photo shoots for this book.

1 2 3 4 5 6 11 10 09 08 07 06

TABLE OF CONTENTS

Training to Tumble 4

CHAPTER 1
The Complete Athlete 6

CHAPTER 2
Training Tips 14

CHAPTER 3
Let's Get Physical 22

8-9

14-15

26-27

Features

Glossary 30

Fast Facts 31

Read More 31

Internet Sites 31

About the Author 32

Index 32

Training to Tumble

Think about your favorite foods. A lot of ingredients work together to make those delicious dishes you crave. Gymnastics training is like a recipe for success. While learning to tumble, gymnasts must improve their balance, strength, **endurance**, and flexibility. If any of those ingredients is missing, the final result just won't "taste" as great!

You might be wondering what types of exercises you can do to become a better gymnast. This book will teach you to **condition** your body safely and successfully. It all starts with stretches and smart self-care. Get ready to go for the gold—on *and* off the floor!

1 The Complete Athlete

Train safely, and you'll be more than just a gymnast!

The world of gymnastics is full of all-around athletes. Experienced gymnasts know how to flip, sprint, tumble, twist, and leap—both on the floor and in mid-air. It may *look* easy, but the truth is that it takes many hours of intense training.

Each event in gymnastics requires different skills. For instance, vaulting requires speed and power. On the balance beam, a gymnast needs focus, balance, and strength. In competitions, you'll often be required to take part in many events. The key to winning is training to be a well-rounded athlete.

Safety First

Our bodies aren't naturally made to flip and somersault. If they were, everyone would be tumbling down the streets! In learning how to do these unnatural movements, athletes must warm up properly and train safely. If they don't, the risk of getting hurt can be very high. Unsafe practices cause more than 86,000 gymnastics-related injuries every year.

To play it safe, always train and practice under the supervision of a trained **spotter** or coach. If something hurts, don't be shy! Tell your coach so that he or she can figure out whether you need to see a doctor. Your health and safety need to come first if you want to finish in first place.

"After a while, if you work on a certain move consistently then it doesn't seem so risky."

–Nadia Comaneci, Romanian Olympic medalist

It's a Stretch

Do you know why preparation for working out is called "warming up?" It's because cold muscles are more likely to get injured or strained—now that's a chilling thought!

You're probably itching to dive right in. But it's important to take 10 to 20 minutes before any gymnastics session to get your muscles ready. Activities like jumping jacks, walking, jogging in place, or stretching will do just that. You can make warm-up time more fun by playing some tunes or doing it with a friend!

Turn the page to find out how to make those muscles toasty warm with some simple stretches.

Kick-start your workout with these easy stretches:

Crisscross

Stand with one leg crossed in front of the other and your feet side by side. Bend forward to touch your toes, and hold for five seconds. Repeat several times, and then do the same with the other leg in front.

Straddle Sit

Sit down with your legs spread out in a V shape in front of you. Turn to one side and reach for your ankle, trying to bring your chin to your knee. Hold for five seconds. Then stretch to the center and the other side. Continue until you've stretched to each place three times.

Leg Lifts

Lie flat on your back and bend your knees, keeping your feet on the ground. Raise one leg in the air. Pull your raised leg toward your face, and hold for 10 seconds. To increase the stretch, straighten your lifted leg. Then, with your lifted leg, alternately point and flex your foot 10 times. Repeat with the other leg.

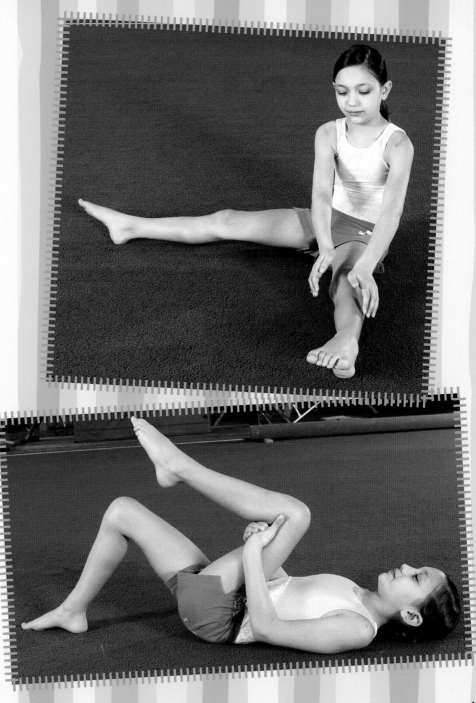

② Training Tips

Star athletes train to build flexibility, strength, endurance, and balance.

Building Flexibility

Say goodbye to stiffness! Fine-tuning your flexibility will reduce your chances of injury. Also, flexible gymnasts are better able to perform skills like splits and toe touches. Here are some great flexibility boosters.

Warm Shoulder

Many moves start from the shoulders, so it's important to keep them limber. Put your arms out to each side and do several sets of small and large circles. Forward and backward shoulder rolls are another surefire method of warming up.

Hippie Chick

The hips are key in tumbling moves like tucks and walkovers. To improve hip flexibility, lie face down on the ground with your arms straight in front of you and your toes pointed. Lift your head, arms, and feet all at once so that your body is shaped like a boat. Hold for at least 10 seconds and then release.

DUAL PURPOSE

The great thing about these moves is you get two workouts in one! Not only do these moves keep you limber, but they also help build strength!

Building Strength

You are gymnast, hear you roar! Strength plays a critical role in being able to do gymnastics skills like headstands and handsprings. In training, the trick for gymnasts is to achieve maximum muscle while keeping a lean body shape. It'd be pretty hard to flip and twist a stocky bodybuilder's figure!

So how can you power up? Try these tips on for size:

* Practice the two "Ps": push-ups and pull-ups! When doing push-ups, keep your body straight and your tummy pulled in. For pull-ups, make sure your legs are straight and kept together.

* You may think the best way to pump up strength would be to lift weights. But many coaches debate whether weight training is useful for gymnasts. If you do lift weights, work with a trainer. He or she can help you build strength without gaining too much bulk.

BUILDING ENDURANCE

Did you know that most floor and beam routines last 90 seconds? This means you have to be prepared to run, tumble, dance, and entertain non-stop during that time! Building up your endurance will keep you from losing steam.

To raise endurance, engage in **cardio** activities that keep your heart rate up. Try aerobics, swimming, and cycling.

Another idea is to try continuous endurance training. This means you run, walk, or jog for 30 to 45 minutes without stopping. The idea isn't to go as fast as you can. Ideally, you should keep a steady, relaxing pace to avoid overworking your body. A test for a good pace is to see if you can chat easily while running. If you can't chat, you're probably going too fast!

"Talent alone is not enough. I believe that a gymnast is 10 percent inspiration and 90 percent perspiration."

—Vladislav Rastorotsky, former Soviet Olympic coach

Building Balance

Balance comes into play while performing skills on the floor and balance beam. The ability to keep your balance comes from the center, or core, of your body. Doing activities that strengthen that area, like **Pilates** or ab workouts, is a very effective way to improve your balance.

Here are some other ideas for building balance:

* Jump rope. For the best balance workout, practice jumping on one foot.

* Put a piece of tape about as long as your foot on the ground. Practice jumping over it quickly from side to side.

* Stand up straight and bend one leg behind you, holding the foot close to your behind for as long as you can.

JUMP FOR JOY

Jumping rope is an exercise that gives you more bang for the buck. In addition to building balance, you get a good cardio workout!

3 Let's Get Physical

Take care of your whole body to be a champion!

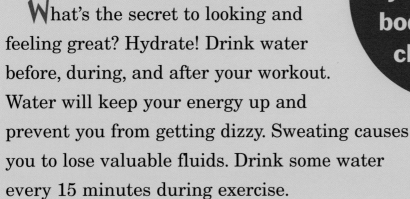

What's the secret to looking and feeling great? Hydrate! Drink water before, during, and after your workout. Water will keep your energy up and prevent you from getting dizzy. Sweating causes you to lose valuable fluids. Drink some water every 15 minutes during exercise.

Just as important as hydrating is fueling up. A good diet will keep you going for hours. Here's a cheat sheet for eating right: eat lots of grains, veggies, fruits, dairy products, meat, and fish. The night before a hard workout, eat a meal rich in **protein** and **carbohydrates**. Foods like pasta, cereal, or chicken will do the trick.

High-Energy Snacks

Between meals, power up with one of these snacks:

almonds
energy bars
fruit
oatmeal
string cheese
trail mix
yogurt

YOGURT

Get in Shape, Girl

All gymnastics, all the time can make you one dull girl! Variety is the spice of life, and gymnastics training is no different. A good mix of exercises is the best way to stay in shape and avoid burnout. The following are some fun ideas for fitness that will keep you on your toes!

Taking **dance classes** is a popular choice for gymnasts because many tumbling routines feature dance moves. Learning to dance will also improve your rhythm, flexibility, and grace.

Running or jogging will help you go the distance in gymnastics! Doing so regularly will increase your speed for tumbling passes and build up your endurance.

Want a crash course in balance? Try your hand (and feet) at in-line skating or ice-skating.

Looking Great, Feeling Great

When looking at competitive gymnasts, one similarity often shows. Their bodies are usually tiny and compact. And though muscular, they are often very thin. It's true that this body type lends itself to performing advanced tumbling skills. But some gymnasts go to dangerous lengths to achieve it. Olympic silver medalist Christy Henrich died in 1994 after battling with **eating disorders**. Her death is a tragic indicator of the pressure many gymnasts feel to stay skinny.

Starving yourself or throwing up after you eat is extremely harmful and doesn't do you any good. If you're concerned about gaining weight, work with your coach to develop a smart nutrition plan. A healthy approach to eating is key for good long-term health and mental well-being. Think like a *real* champion: honor your body and accept your body type!

Regimens of the Fit and Famous

Are you prepared to spend as many as 35 to 50 hours per week at the gym? Competitive gymnasts often spend at least that much time training in preparation for regional, national, and international events. Daily practices are filled with drills, personal instruction, stretching, and work on the **apparatus.**

In her book *Dominique Moceanu: An American Champion*, Olympic medalist Dominique Moceanu detailed her rigid training routine. Waking up around 6 a.m. each morning, Moceanu would head to a three-hour practice. Lunch and physical therapy followed, and then another three-hour practice. Sleep and homework filled in the rare blanks!

Even if you never have dreams of Olympic medals, keeping your body in shape is important. Proper training and practice will make you a star at any level!

Dominique Moceanu

"My attitude is never to be satisfied, never enough, never."
—Bela Karolyi, former U.S. Olympic coach

Glossary

apparatus (ap-uh-RAT-uhss)—equipment used in gymnastics, such as the balance beam or uneven bars

carbohydrate (kar-boh-HYE-drate)—a substance found in foods such as bread, rice, cereal, and potatoes that gives you energy

cardio (KAR-dee-oh)—having to do with the heart; cardio activities work the heart and keep it healthy.

condition (kuhn-DISH-uhn)—to train your body to be better able to handle the demands of fitness and sports

eating disorder (EET-ing dis-OR-dur)—a medical issue in which someone has a distorted view of his or her body and develops dangerous eating habits to lose weight

endurance (en-DUR-uhnss)—the ability to handle long periods of exercise

Pilates (puh-LAHT-eez)—a type of exercise that uses controlled movements to strengthen muscles, focusing on the muscles of the core

protein (PROH-teen)—a substance found in foods such as meat, cheese, eggs, and fish

spotter (SPOT-tur)—a trained professional who watches and helps gymnasts for safety reasons

Fast Facts

* In 1811, Frederick Jahn opened the first modern gymnastics center. His students used gymnastics as a way to train for other sports. Today, gymnastics is its own sport.

* Train hard enough, and you just might become the most decorated gymnast. Russian gymnast Larissa Latynina holds that honor with 18 Olympic medals.

Read More

Morley, Christine. *The Best Book of Gymnastics.* New York: Kingfisher, 2003.

Wesley, Ann. *Competitive Gymnastics for Girls.* Sports Girl. New York: Rosen, 2001.

Internet Sites

FactHound offers a safe, fun way to find Internet sites related to this book. All of the sites on FactHound have been researched by our staff.

Here's how:

1. Visit *www.facthound.com*

2. Choose your grade level.

3. Type in this book ID **0736864717** for age-appropriate sites. You may also browse subjects by clicking on letters, or by clicking on pictures and words.

4. Click on the **Fetch It** button.

Facthound will fetch the best sites for you!

About the Author

Jen Jones has been very involved in the cheerleading and gymnastics worlds since she was old enough to turn a cartwheel! Jen has several years of gymnastics training and spent seven years as a cheerleader. After college, Jen cheered and choreographed for the Chicago Lawmen semi-professional football dance team. Today Jen lives in Los Angeles and writes for publications like *Pilates Style*, *American Cheerleader*, and *Dance Spirit*. She also teaches cheerleading, dance, and Pilates classes and is a certified BalleCore instructor.

Index

ab workouts, 20
aerobics, 18

balance, 4, 6, 20, 21, 25
body type, 26–27

cardio activities, 18, 21

dancing, 24
diet, 22, 23, 27

endurance, 4, 18, 25

flexibility, 4, 14–15, 24

jogging, 10, 18, 25

nutrition, 22, 27

Pilates, 20
pull-ups, 16
push-ups, 16

running, 18, 25

safety, 8
skating, 25
spotters, 8
strength, 4, 6, 15, 16
stretching, 10, 12–13

training time, 6, 28

warming up, 8, 10, 12–13, 14
water, 22
weight training, 16